All The Reasons *NOT* To Use SPEAKER BUREAUS

All The Reasons *NOT* To Use SPEAKER BUREAUS

A Comprehensive Look At All The Advantages Of Booking Speakers Without The Help Of A Professional

Jeff Slutsky

With Nancy Lauterbach

All The Reasons NOT to Use Speaker Bureaus
By Jeff Slutsky, with Nancy Lauterbach

For info on booking Jeff Slutsky contact:
Nancy Lauterbach • O: 480.366.4040 • C: 913.488.6480 • nancy@redprops.com

10 9 8 7 6 5 4 3 2 1 Blast Off

ISBN-13: 978-1496176981
ISBN-10: 1496176987

Dedication

This book is dedicated to all the hard working agents and bureaus who book professional speakers, like Jeff Slutsky.
(Yes, I'm sucking up.)

OTHER BOOKS BY JEFF SLUTSKY

To order books - https://www.allthereasons.net

THIS PAGE IS ALSO BLANK DUE TO LACK OF REASONS

THIS PAGE IS BLANK
DUE TO LACK OF REASONS

THIS PAGE IS ALSO BLANK
DUE TO LACK OF REASONS

THIS PAGE IS BLANK
DUE TO LACK OF REASONS

THIS PAGE IS ALSO BLANK DUE TO LACK OF REASONS

THIS PAGE IS BLANK
DUE TO LACK OF REASONS

THIS PAGE IS ALSO BLANK
DUE TO LACK OF REASONS

8   Jeff Slutsky

THIS PAGE IS BLANK
DUE TO LACK OF REASONS

THIS PAGE IS ALSO BLANK DUE TO LACK OF REASONS

THIS PAGE IS BLANK
DUE TO LACK OF REASONS

THIS PAGE IS ALSO BLANK DUE TO LACK OF REASONS

THIS PAGE IS BLANK
DUE TO LACK OF REASONS

THIS PAGE IS ALSO BLANK
DUE TO LACK OF REASONS

THIS PAGE IS BLANK
DUE TO LACK OF REASONS

THIS PAGE IS ALSO BLANK
DUE TO LACK OF REASONS

THIS PAGE IS BLANK
DUE TO LACK OF REASONS

THIS PAGE IS ALSO BLANK
DUE TO LACK OF REASONS

THIS PAGE IS BLANK DUE TO LACK OF REASONS

THIS PAGE IS ALSO BLANK
DUE TO LACK OF REASONS

THIS PAGE IS BLANK
DUE TO LACK OF REASONS

THIS PAGE IS ALSO BLANK
DUE TO LACK OF REASONS

THIS PAGE IS BLANK
DUE TO LACK OF REASONS

THIS PAGE IS ALSO BLANK
DUE TO LACK OF REASONS

THIS PAGE IS BLANK
DUE TO LACK OF REASONS

THIS PAGE IS ALSO BLANK
DUE TO LACK OF REASONS

THIS PAGE IS BLANK
DUE TO LACK OF REASONS

THIS PAGE IS ALSO BLANK DUE TO LACK OF REASONS

THIS PAGE IS BLANK
DUE TO LACK OF REASONS

THIS PAGE IS ALSO BLANK
DUE TO LACK OF REASONS

THIS PAGE IS BLANK
DUE TO LACK OF REASONS

THIS PAGE IS ALSO BLANK
DUE TO LACK OF REASONS

THIS PAGE IS BLANK
DUE TO LACK OF REASONS

THIS PAGE IS ALSO BLANK
DUE TO LACK OF REASONS

THIS PAGE IS BLANK
DUE TO LACK OF REASONS

THIS PAGE IS ALSO BLANK
DUE TO LACK OF REASONS

THIS PAGE IS BLANK
DUE TO LACK OF REASONS

THIS PAGE IS ALSO BLANK
DUE TO LACK OF REASONS

THIS PAGE IS BLANK
DUE TO LACK OF REASONS

THIS PAGE IS ALSO BLANK
DUE TO LACK OF REASONS

THIS PAGE IS BLANK
DUE TO LACK OF REASONS

THIS PAGE IS ALSO BLANK
DUE TO LACK OF REASONS

THIS PAGE IS BLANK
DUE TO LACK OF REASONS

THIS PAGE IS ALSO BLANK
DUE TO LACK OF REASONS

THIS PAGE IS BLANK
DUE TO LACK OF REASONS

THIS PAGE IS ALSO BLANK
DUE TO LACK OF REASONS

THIS PAGE IS BLANK
DUE TO LACK OF REASONS

THIS PAGE IS ALSO BLANK
DUE TO LACK OF REASONS

THIS PAGE IS BLANK
DUE TO LACK OF REASONS

THIS PAGE IS ALSO BLANK
DUE TO LACK OF REASONS

THIS PAGE IS BLANK
DUE TO LACK OF REASONS

THIS PAGE IS ALSO BLANK
DUE TO LACK OF REASONS

THIS PAGE IS BLANK
DUE TO LACK OF REASONS

THIS PAGE IS ALSO BLANK
DUE TO LACK OF REASONS

THIS PAGE IS BLANK
DUE TO LACK OF REASONS

THIS PAGE IS ALSO BLANK DUE TO LACK OF REASONS

THIS PAGE IS BLANK
DUE TO LACK OF REASONS

THIS PAGE IS ALSO BLANK DUE TO LACK OF REASONS

THIS PAGE IS BLANK
DUE TO LACK OF REASONS

THIS PAGE IS ALSO BLANK
DUE TO LACK OF REASONS

JEFF SLUTSKY

THIS PAGE IS BLANK
DUE TO LACK OF REASONS

THIS PAGE IS ALSO BLANK
DUE TO LACK OF REASONS

THIS PAGE IS BLANK
DUE TO LACK OF REASONS

THIS PAGE IS ALSO BLANK
DUE TO LACK OF REASONS

THIS PAGE IS BLANK
DUE TO LACK OF REASONS

THIS PAGE IS ALSO BLANK
DUE TO LACK OF REASONS

THIS PAGE IS BLANK
DUE TO LACK OF REASONS

THIS PAGE IS ALSO BLANK
DUE TO LACK OF REASONS

THIS PAGE IS BLANK
DUE TO LACK OF REASONS

THIS PAGE IS ALSO BLANK
DUE TO LACK OF REASONS

THIS PAGE IS BLANK
DUE TO LACK OF REASONS

THIS PAGE IS ALSO BLANK
DUE TO LACK OF REASONS

THIS PAGE IS BLANK
DUE TO LACK OF REASONS

THIS PAGE IS ALSO BLANK
DUE TO LACK OF REASONS

THIS PAGE IS BLANK
DUE TO LACK OF REASONS

THIS PAGE IS ALSO BLANK
DUE TO LACK OF REASONS

THIS PAGE IS BLANK
DUE TO LACK OF REASONS

THIS PAGE IS ALSO BLANK
DUE TO LACK OF REASONS

THIS PAGE IS BLANK
DUE TO LACK OF REASONS

THIS PAGE IS ALSO BLANK
DUE TO LACK OF REASONS

THIS PAGE IS BLANK
DUE TO LACK OF REASONS

THIS PAGE IS ALSO BLANK
DUE TO LACK OF REASONS

THIS PAGE IS BLANK
DUE TO LACK OF REASONS

THIS PAGE IS ALSO BLANK
DUE TO LACK OF REASONS

THIS PAGE IS BLANK
DUE TO LACK OF REASONS

THIS PAGE IS ALSO BLANK
DUE TO LACK OF REASONS

THIS PAGE IS BLANK
DUE TO LACK OF REASONS

THIS PAGE IS ALSO BLANK
DUE TO LACK OF REASONS

THIS PAGE IS BLANK
DUE TO LACK OF REASONS

THIS PAGE IS ALSO BLANK
DUE TO LACK OF REASONS

THIS PAGE IS BLANK DUE TO LACK OF REASONS

THIS PAGE IS ALSO BLANK
DUE TO LACK OF REASONS

THIS PAGE IS BLANK
DUE TO LACK OF REASONS

THIS PAGE IS ALSO BLANK
DUE TO LACK OF REASONS

THIS PAGE IS BLANK
DUE TO LACK OF REASONS

THIS PAGE IS ALSO BLANK DUE TO LACK OF REASONS

THIS PAGE IS BLANK
DUE TO LACK OF REASONS

THIS PAGE IS ALSO BLANK
DUE TO LACK OF REASONS

THIS PAGE IS BLANK
DUE TO LACK OF REASONS

THIS PAGE IS ALSO BLANK
DUE TO LACK OF REASONS

THIS PAGE IS BLANK
DUE TO LACK OF REASONS

THIS PAGE IS ALSO BLANK
DUE TO LACK OF REASONS

THIS PAGE IS BLANK
DUE TO LACK OF REASONS

THIS PAGE IS ALSO BLANK
DUE TO LACK OF REASONS

THIS PAGE IS BLANK
DUE TO LACK OF REASONS

THIS PAGE IS ALSO BLANK
DUE TO LACK OF REASONS

THIS PAGE IS BLANK
DUE TO LACK OF REASONS

THIS PAGE IS ALSO BLANK
DUE TO LACK OF REASONS

THIS PAGE IS BLANK
DUE TO LACK OF REASONS

THIS PAGE IS ALSO BLANK
DUE TO LACK OF REASONS

THIS PAGE IS BLANK
DUE TO LACK OF REASONS

THIS PAGE IS ALSO BLANK
DUE TO LACK OF REASONS

THIS PAGE IS BLANK
DUE TO LACK OF REASONS

THIS PAGE IS ALSO BLANK
DUE TO LACK OF REASONS

THIS PAGE IS BLANK
DUE TO LACK OF REASONS

THIS PAGE IS ALSO BLANK
DUE TO LACK OF REASONS

THIS PAGE IS BLANK
DUE TO LACK OF REASONS

THIS PAGE IS ALSO BLANK
DUE TO LACK OF REASONS

THIS PAGE IS BLANK
DUE TO LACK OF REASONS

THIS PAGE IS ALSO BLANK
DUE TO LACK OF REASONS

THIS PAGE IS BLANK
DUE TO LACK OF REASONS

THIS PAGE IS ALSO BLANK
DUE TO LACK OF REASONS

THIS PAGE IS BLANK
DUE TO LACK OF REASONS

THIS PAGE IS ALSO BLANK
DUE TO LACK OF REASONS

THIS PAGE IS BLANK
DUE TO LACK OF REASONS

THIS PAGE IS ALSO BLANK
DUE TO LACK OF REASONS

To order more copies of this book on line:

https://www.allthereasons.net

Also Available:

Books with a simple message and a big impact!
https://www.allthereasons.net

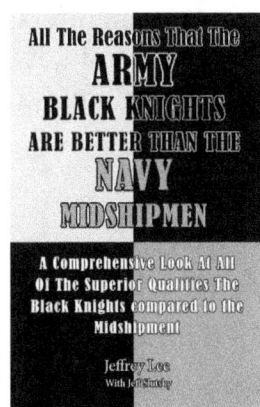

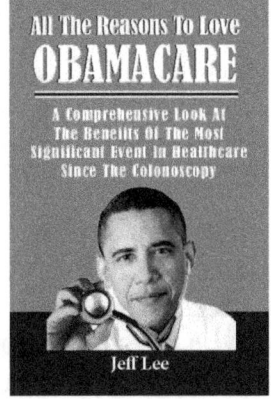

Your Clients Can Get Their Own, Custom "Book" When They Book Slutsky

Imagine your client's audience response when, during this game-changing and funny keynote, Jeff Slutsky introduces his new book with your client's name in the title! Then, everybody gets their own copy, where they soon discover it's 141 blank pages. That's because there are NO reasons NOT to take full advantage of the superior quality and service your client offers! And that's just one of several key messages that they'll take away, (along with the book).

Your Own Custom Book Cover And since there are no reasons and no excuses...there are 141 Blank Pages!

JEFF KEYNOTED AT THE ZEN WINDOWS ANNUAL FRANCHISEE CONVENTION. THE RESPONSE TO THE BOOK WAS OVERWHELMING.

Slutsky's Most Popular Smart Topics:
Smart Leadership: Executing the strategy with savvy.
Smart Selling: Easy tactics to get the buy or the buy-in.
Smart Marketing: Results on a shoestring budget.
Smart Communication: The Influence Booster.

Getting More From Your People Has Never Been More Fun! With Jeff Slutsky's Hilarious Motivational

"This is the fourth time we've worked with Jeff and he was better than ever! Very funny, great content, engaging and easy to work with."

-- Michael Jeffreys, CEO, Seminars on Demand

Give Your Success A Shot In The Arm with Slutsky's
INFLUENCE BOOSTER ®

Jeff Slutsky's new, maximum strength motivational speech, is infused with all-natural street-savvy ideas and hilarious anecdotes that empowers your people to succeed during these hyper stressful times. Let Slutsky immunize your attendees from results-deficiency and anemic performance. While laughter may be the best medicine, today's environment demands that humor be enhanced with equal parts: content, audience interaction and practical, proven ideas for those who suffer from mild to moderate apathy. That's why the new and improved, INFLUENCE BOOSTER keynote speech, is now available without a prescription and ready to be administered at your meeting or convention. Ask your meeting planner if Slutsky's INFLUENCE BOOSTER is right for you. Use only as directed.

Call or Email Today for Fees and Availabilities

Nancy Lauterbach • O:480.366.4040 • C:913.488.6480 • nancy@redprops.com
Bill Lauterbach • office: 480.366.4040 • cell: 913.706.0241 • bill@redprops.com
Kathy Popplewell Morris • office: (425) 221-1728 • kathy@redprops.com

www.ingramcontent.com/pod-product-compliance
Lightning Source LLC
Chambersburg PA
CBHW051715170526
45167CB00002B/671